CW01604755

THE NEW LIFE LIB

INSTANT MEDITATION

FOR STRESS RELIEF

THE NEW LIFE LIBRARY

INSTANT MEDITATION

FOR STRESS RELIEF

BREATHING TECHNIQUES AND MENTAL EXERCISES FOR AN IMMEDIATE SENSE OF CALM AND WELL-BEING

JOHN HUDSON

SELECT EDITIONS

Select Editions imprint specially produced for
Selectabook Ltd

Produced by Anness Publishing Limited

Hermes House, 88-89 Blackfriars Road,
London SE1 8HA

A CIP catalogue record for this book is available from the British Library

ISBN 1 84081 475 6

Publisher: Joanna Lorenz
Editor: Fiona Eaton
Designer: Bobbie Colgate Stone
Illustrator: Giovanna Pierce
Jacket Photographer: Don Last

Printed and bound in Singapore

1 3 5 7 9 10 8 6 4 2

Contents

What is Meditation?

Meditation has been in use from the beginning of time: people have always sought inner quiet and physical relaxation, for spiritual, self-realization or health reasons. It is nothing unusual and you do not have to be a physical contortionist to be able to achieve and enjoy the benefits of meditation at both physical and mental levels.

What, then, is meditation? As one speaker put it recently, it is just sitting and relaxing. Many people find that their lives are so full of the demands of work, family, friends and organized leisure pursuits that they have no time to "stand and stare". Many are so caught up in planning and working towards the future that they take little pleasure from the here and now. In their bustle to "get on" they miss out on the simple pleasures of life; the change of the seasons, the singing of a bird, or the innocent wonder of a child. But beauty and joy are there to be seen and experienced, even in the most industrial of landscapes. Meditation can be a good way of just taking time out, and allowing yourself to tune into and appreciate the moment. It may be walking along the seashore, or

sitting by a stream, or just noticing the intensity of silence in a still room and enjoying it.

Rather than pushing yourself to take up some strained physical position, just relax; sit in a chair or stroll in a favourite landscape at a steady pace. It is not a good idea to slump or lie down, as this only tends to lead into sleep. It is a relaxed attentiveness that is desired. If you sit down, do so with your feet flat on the floor, hands resting in your lap or on the arms of the chair, and your head comfortably balanced. If you are walking, do so slowly and carefully, aware of the movement of each foot, and the contact with the ground beneath. One recollection is of a Buddhist monk in Sri Lanka walking up and down the same path in the forest; he moved slowly, giving total attention to his feet, the movement of his feet, changing pressures on the soles of his feet, and the reaction of the ground to his feet. This is an extremely simple but effective exercise in being truly aware of the present.

Meditation, above all, is about staying with the moment, being in touch with one's surroundings and one's inner world, much of which is more easily accessible when in the meditative state.

Left: Meditation can help you to reach your inner responses to the world around you. Right: If you are walking, be aware of the changing pressures on the soles of your feet.

Notice the varied textures of every surface you walk on.

A common misunderstanding about meditation is that it is confined to the eastern religions. As we shall see, meditation has been used in most of the world's religions in one form or another, and for many it is a religious experience promoting spiritual awareness. However, it is also a technique that can be utilized for its therapeutic and relaxing benefits in stress management, or simply in pursuit of self-awareness.

Meditation is a pleasant way to gain deep relaxation with time and space to yourself. Just meditating on a regular basis can be beneficial, but using some simple words and images while you meditate can promote an improvement in your general well-being or in a specific area of your life, or help you to gain the confidence to cope with an event in the future. This book is designed to provide you with an introduction to meditation and its usefulness in all these ways, as concisely and simply as possible.

Meditation is for everyone who wishes to relax and enjoy their own inner peace.

How Often to Meditate?

The benefits of meditation come from regular use. If you are under stress, you may find that meditating twice daily will be effective in restoring composure and reducing irritability. Make a time and space you can call your own and use breathing and relaxation exercises to ease yourself into the meditative state. The more you practise meditation the less time you will need to spend on these, but they remain useful in calming and preparing you. Allow at least ten, ideally 20, minutes in meditation at each session.

Right: Walking, or simply being, in a place surrounded by natural colour, movement and sound can be a truly meditative experience.

History of Meditation

Meditation is perhaps most closely linked with Buddhism, and indeed it was the main practice through which its founder, Gautama, finally gained enlightenment. Buddhism has defined many stages of meditation that are practised in order to achieve the ultimate level of purifying the mind and clearing away of all thoughts and mental images.

However, one of the best-known practices of meditation is yoga, the yoking or harnessing of mental and physical powers, which is very much in the Hindu tradition. Most of us think in terms of "hatha" or royal yoga, which is a series of physical exercises and postures performed to gain physical, and therefore mental, control. Less well-known is "bhakti" yoga, which is focusing of the mind, and is akin to the style of meditation outlined here and indeed practised in the Christian faith. According to this discipline, the

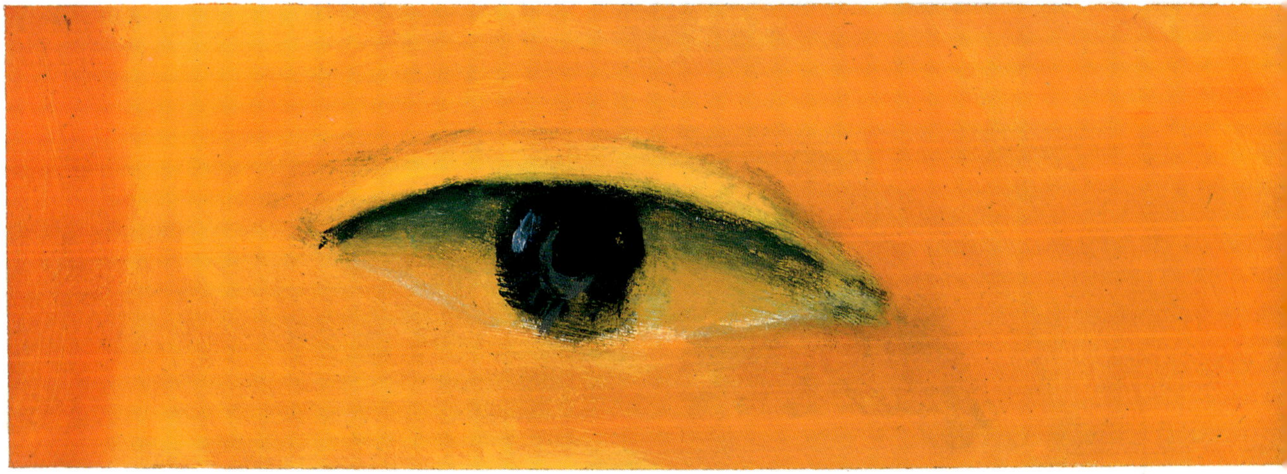

practitioner sits and focuses his or her attention upon an aspect of their god. In so doing, they gain insights into their own responses to the knowledge they have of that god's powers and the lessons to be drawn from stories told of him or her.

It has long been a tradition in Christian religious communities, such as convents and monasteries, for monks or nuns to spend a period of time each day in quiet contemplation, often focusing upon a crucifix and contemplating the passion of Christ and all that it means for the believer. This is, of course, meditation, and has all the benefits of helping the individual come to an understanding of his inner beliefs and response to his faith. The practice has also become increasingly popular among lay Christians in recent years.

Right: Meditation is a part of all the world's religions. Left and below: Representations of the Buddha, which worshippers use as a focus for meditation.

THE MENTAL AND PHYSICAL BENEFITS OF MEDITATION

An individual emerging from a period of meditation, however brief, will notice a change in their emotional state from when they started their meditation exercise. This can present itself in many ways, often as a feeling of being refreshed, with a more positive attitude and a general feeling of well-being. Things that had been bothering them may now be seen in a new and more helpful way. They have a different perspective on things and feel much more in control.

These reactions have been known for years, but only in recent times has a physiological explanation been available. Knowledge gained from brain scans and the measurement of brain wave patterns has given new information about the "alpha state".

When we are truly relaxed, both mentally and physically, there are changes in the brain wave pattern until it is predominantly within the alpha state. Within this state the brain triggers chemicals known as

Left: Mind and body work together in meditation to promote health and well-being in the whole person.

endorphins. It is this chemical trigger that has the benefits that are experienced as a feeling of well-being. Indeed, endorphins have been called "nature's own opiates". Meditation is one of the easiest ways to achieve this, and these good feelings can continue for some time after the meditation has ended, the length of time varying with each individual.

There is also a very real physical benefit, as these same endorphins also boost the immune system, thus helping the person to fight off infection and maintain good health.

Below: The change in brain wave patterns as a result of regular meditation can give you a feeling of alert calmness and increased mental composure. You may feel as if you are back in control again.

MEDITATION WITHIN THE CONTEXT OF A BUSY WORK LIFE

As mentioned earlier, the tensions of modern working practices often mean that people are so bound up in meeting all the demands placed upon them that they maintain a high level of mental and physical activity throughout their waking hours. This frequently means that they are not only cutting off their emotional responses and their enjoyment of the simple things in life, but are also pushing their physical and mental health to the limit. Much has now been written about stress management, and the many books on the subject emphasize the need for a period of mental and physical relaxation at different stages in the day. They point out that by taking this time out one actually gains rather than loses when it comes to productivity, as the brain simply cannot maintain intense activity for long periods and remain efficient.

Stress can become damaging when we can no longer control our responses to it.

One writer, Ernest Rossi, has formulated the "20-minute rule", which is based on the theory of ultradian rhythms. Ultradian rhythms are biorhythms that the body works through during each day – a little like hyperbolic curves of energy which repeat every 90 to 120 minutes or so. Naturally, it would be best to work only at peak performance times, but this is just not possible. However, timing your work breaks to coincide with the mind/body slow-down pattern every 90 minutes ensures maximum productivity and restricts the build-up of stress.

Rossi suggested, and indeed practises, the pattern of working for 90 minutes and then taking a

20-minute break. He usually lies down and meditates in this period, as it is the best form of total mental and physical relaxation and good preparation for returning to optimum mental processing.

It is important that these breaks take place every 90 minutes or so, in such a way as to completely change the mind/body state. Ideally, you should stop all work activity and experience a change of physical status (standing rather than sitting, looking into the distance rather than close up, for example) and mental focus. A 20-minute meditation is ideal and the benefits will be felt immediately.

On returning to work after that 20 minutes, you will see things afresh and deal with them more quickly and efficiently, as the mind and body are alert and ready to climb up to peak performance again on the biorhythmic curve. The feeling of well-being will continue well into the next 90-minute period.

Is it coincidence that workers throughout the world have evolved breaks at approximately 90-minute intervals (coffee – lunch – tea)? This has grown up through experience, and has occurred in all types of work environment. Unfortunately, the intense demands of modern work practices, instant communication, and rising numbers of self-employed workers have meant that more and more people have found it convenient to take their breaks at the desk, or to ignore breaks altogether. It is a false economy, based on the premise that one can keep going indefinitely, and in fact, it leads to greater inefficiency and is harmful to both the worker and their work.

Left: Be aware of your biological clock throughout the working day and try to take a break every 90 minutes.

Exercises for Physical Relaxation

The first essential in approaching the meditative state is to learn to relax fully. When you stop working, the tension that has built up in your mind and body remains and must be diffused before you can truly begin to benefit from a period of rest. A programme of exercises will loosen contracted muscles and make you feel refreshed, revitalized and physically relaxed. As well as unwinding the stresses in your body, exercise has the added benefit of releasing mental tension, so it can be a helpful prelude to every meditation session.

If strains and tensions are allowed to build up in the body they may lead on to a variety of aches and pains, as well as increasing mental strain and diminishing coordination and efficiency.

A single session of exercises for relaxation will immediately refresh and calm you. Loosening your muscles will also make you aware of areas of tension in your body, so that you can give some attention to sorting out the causes: improving your posture, the way you sit at your desk, or the shoes you wear.

Just as tension produces an arousal response, relaxation has the opposite effect on the body, reducing not only muscular tension but also rates of respiration and digestion, blood pressure and heart rate, while increasing the efficiency of the internal organs and the immune system.

While it is vital to relieve tension when you feel it building up into aching or stiffness, it is better to avoid such a build-up by incorporating relaxation exercises into your daily routine. Use them to stretch stiff muscles when you get up in the morning, or during a mid-morning or 20-minute afternoon break from work. At bedtime, taking a few minutes to release tension in your neck, back and shoulders will aid sound, relaxing sleep. Training your body to relax fully will calm your mind and prepare it for the meditative state.

Relax in a position that is comfortable for you.

Relaxation Exercises for Neck, Back and Shoulders

1 Stand upright with your arms stretched above your head. Lift up on to your toes and stretch further still.

2 Drop forward, keeping your knees relaxed, and let your arms, head and shoulders hang heavy and loose for a while.

3 Shake out your head and arms, then slowly return to standing. Repeat a few times.

Sitting Relaxation Exercises for Neck, Back and Shoulders

1 Sit upright in a firm chair with your lower back supported and your feet squarely on the floor, hip-width apart. Raise your arms above your head and stretch them upwards, feeling the pull in your upper body. Look upwards and hold the stretch.

2 Drop forward, letting your head and arms relax completely. Return to the starting position and repeat the exercise, staying aware of the changing tensions in the muscles.

3 To stretch the back, link your hands together over the top of the chair, and lift your arms slightly. Lean back gradually, arching your back over the chair, hold, then repeat.

Alternate Nostril Breathing

1 Concentrating your attention on regular, quiet breathing is both physically calming and helps to clear your mind of any intrusive thoughts as an aid to meditation. Place the first two fingers of one hand on your forehead, with thumb and third finger reaching down on either side of your nose.

2 Relax your thumb and inhale through that nostril; pinch it closed again, then release the finger to exhale through the other nostril.

◄ **3** Breathe in on the same side, then close that nostril and breathe out on the other side. Continue to breathe slowly through alternate nostrils.

Rhythmic Breathing

To most of us breathing is a totally mechanical act, but at times of stress we often breathe incorrectly. Practise these exercises to become aware of each breath and to help your breathing become more rhythmical and steady. Stop if you feel dizzy, and never force your breath.

Postures for Meditation

Meditation is a very personal experience and you can meditate anywhere that suits you – on the bus, along a beach, at home. It is important for you to find a position in which to meditate that feels comfortable for you. You should feel relaxed without drifting off to sleep, and you should be able to remain still for the period of meditation without experiencing any numbness or cramp in your limbs that would be distracting. Experiment with the following suggestions until you find what feels best for you.

Sitting on the Floor

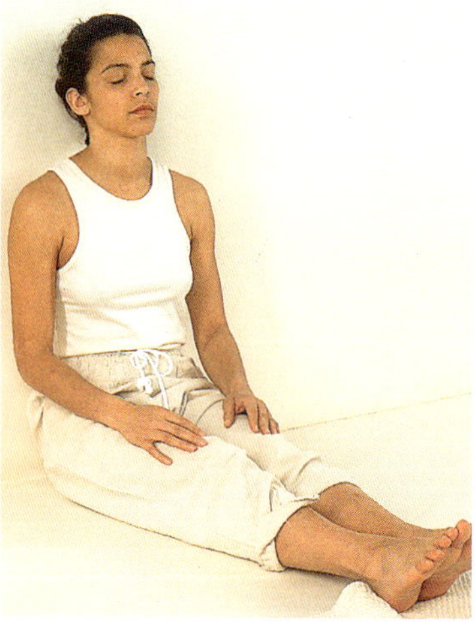

Sit with your back straight and supported by the wall with your legs outstretched and feet together. Rest your hands on your thighs.

Sitting on a Chair

Choose a firm chair that supports your lower back well. Put your feet together, resting flat on the floor, and rest your hands on your thighs. Keep your back straight but your shoulders relaxed, and your head up.

Sitting on your Heels

This posture is a good one for your back as it keeps the spine straight. The feet should be relaxed with the toes pointing backwards. Use a cushion under your feet if you wish. Rest your hands lightly on your lap.

The Lotus Position

1 The half-lotus is the simpler version: bend one leg so that the foot rests on the opposite inner thigh. Place the second foot on top of the thigh of the first leg. Keep the spine upright and rest the hands lightly on the knees.

2 For the full lotus, the first leg should be bent with the foot on top of the other thigh, and the second leg then bent so that the foot goes over the other leg on to the opposite thigh.

Lying Down

Lie flat on your back with the whole of your spine in contact with the floor. Then relax your shoulders and neck. This position has the disadvantage that it may cause you to drift off to sleep.

Ways of Gaining the Meditative State: Sounds

Many religious groups, as well as adherents of Transcendental Meditation, talk of using a sound, or "mantra" to help with meditation, and indeed this can be helpful. The constant repetition of a phrase, a word or sound ("aum" is commonly used in Hinduism) creates the alpha state by an almost hypnotic focus of attention upon the sound. The Hare Krishna movement is well-known for its repetitive chant that is repeated over and over again, and can lead to its members seeming to become "high" – again the effects of endorphin release.

An effortless sound, repeated with the natural rhythm of breathing, can have the same soothing, mentally liberating effect as the constant natural sound of running water, rustling leaves or a beating heart. The single sound, or mantra as it is known, is used to blot out the "chatter" of intrusive thoughts, allowing the mind to find repose. Speaking or chanting a mantra as a stream of endless sound is a very ancient method of heightening a person's awareness by concentrating the senses. The simple gentle sound "om", or "aum", is sometimes known as the first mantra, which is literally an instrument of thought. The curving Sanskrit (the ancient language of Hindus in India) symbol for this primordial word represents the various states of consciousness: waking, dreaming, deep dreamless sleep and the transcendental state.

The Sanskrit symbol that represents the sound "aum".

However, the sound need not be a special word, or incantation; something simple and meaningful will be as, if not more, effective. The sound of the word "calm" spoken or thought with each breath breathed out can be very, very effective, especially while imagining tension leaving your body and a calmness developing. The word "relax" seems to match other people's needs in a similar way. Any word that appeals to you will do, repeated with the flow of breath, silently in the mind, or out loud. This clears the mind, slows the breathing and allows relaxation, both mental and physical, to develop.

USING TOUCH

You can use your sense of touch in a lulling, soothing way to induce a state of meditation when you are under stress. Young children do this when they adopt a satisfyingly smooth ribbon or piece of fabric to hold and manipulate when they are feeling tense.

The same technique can commonly be seen all over the Middle East, where strings of worry beads are rhythmically passed through the fingers at difficult moments to focus the mind and calm anxiety. Their uniform size, gentle round shapes, smooth surfaces and rhythmic, orderly clicking as they are passed along their string all assist the meditative state. Use one or two smooth, rounded stones in the same way, passing them from hand to hand, and concentrating on their temperature, shape and surfaces, or find an object with a tactile quality that particularly appeals to you.

Worry beads.

The constant, yet variable sound of running water can be especially soothing.

Colours

Some colours are associated with relaxation and can be a helpful way to clear the mind of tension and allow meditation to start.

Sit with your eyes closed, and be aware of the colour that comes into your mind: it may be any colour of the rainbow – red or purple are common. Then slowly and gradually allow that colour to change to a blue or green colour, allowing it to fill the whole of your mind's eye and replacing all other colours. The colour pink is also recommended by colour therapists and this may prove helpful. You will find a feeling of relaxation growing as the new colour builds in your mind, and when the relaxed colour is complete, you will experience those pleasant feelings of inner peace and stillness associated with meditation.

Breathing in Colour

You can help the colour to build up by associating it with your breathing. Establish a comfortable rhythm of breathing and focus on it until your mind is clear. Allow your colour to fill your mind's eye, then, as you breathe in, imagine the colour filling your body, from the soles of your feet up to the top of your head.

Colours are associated with various qualities, so choose a colour to suit your individual needs. Red: vitality, energy, strength and willpower (complementary colour turquoise). Orange: happiness and laughter (complementary colour blue). Yellow: intellect and objectivity (complementary colour violet). Green: cleansing and harmony (complementary colour magenta). Turquoise: strengthens the immune system, counteracts disease (complementary colour red). Blue: peace and relaxation, restful sleep (complementary colour orange). Violet: beauty, dignity, self-respect (complementary colour yellow). Magenta: release of obsessional thoughts and memories (complementary colour green).

Make sure you are sitting comfortably - a cushion may help - and breathe in the colour of your choice.

Colour Visualization Exercise

Close your eyes and breathe calmly and regularly, focusing on the rhythm of your breathing. As you inhale, imagine that you are sitting on a beautiful lawn in a peaceful garden. Sense the cool freshness of the green stretching around you. As you breathe out, imagine the velvety magenta of a full-blown rose. Breathe in again and let the balanced, cleansing green fill your mind. Repeat a few times, then sit quietly for a few moments.

Try to become aware of the wonderful colours of the natural world, such as in this field of lavender.

Below: Take in colour with each relaxed breath until the colours permeate your whole being and you feel immersed in colour.

Simple Guided Programmes

You may find it helpful to record the following meditation exercises on to tape, so that you can concentrate on gaining the images, or focusing attention, without worrying about forgetting a passage or having to refer to the page. When recording, just use your normal voice, speaking quite slowly but not drawing out the words in any unnatural way, speaking steadily and quietly, leaving pauses (indicated in the text by ". . .") to allow the mind to develop the image before moving on. You will soon find what feels comfortable for you. It is really very easy and leaves you free to enjoy the feelings and concentration that develops. It can be helpful to have some music in the background on the tape, or indeed while you do the exercises when you have committed them to memory, or when you have developed your own. When choosing music, select something non-intrusive and without sudden changes in speed or pitch.

Physical Relaxation

Sit in a comfortable position, with your hands resting loosely in your lap or on the arms of the chair and your head balanced comfortably; let your eyes close and begin to relax.

First, think of the top of your own head, your scalp, and let all the muscles, skin and nerve-endings there . . . just relax and let go.

Thinking of your facial muscles, just tense them and scrunch them all up: around the eyes, the forehead, around the mouth, scowling and grimacing for a count of five seconds, then release and let go. Feel that relaxation in all those muscle groups; feel all the muscle groups beautifully relaxed and at ease. This may mean your mouth is slightly open, but choose whatever position is best and most comfortable for you . . . just allow it to happen. The more you physically relax the more you'll mentally relax too, so that soon . . . very soon, you can enjoy that pleasant feeling of half-sleep.

Thinking down through the neck and shoulder muscles . . . and on into the tops of your arms, allow

Sitting quietly and comfortably in your special place is a form of meditation.

those muscles to sag down, become tension-free. Thinking of the muscles of the upper arms, tense those muscles for a count of five and let them go, let them relax . . . down into the elbows and on to the forearms, just letting all those areas relax and let go. Down through the wrists . . . into the hands . . . clench your fists really tight for a count of five, then release, releasing any tension and leaving the hands and arms heavy, easy and relaxed.

Think for a moment about your breathing; you're breathing easily and evenly now, so you can let any tension in the chest area drain away, as you think down into the tummy muscles, letting them relax too.

Think down into all the muscles of your back and the muscles down either side of the spine. Allow those muscles to let go; relax and feel good . . . allowing the chair to take all the weight and all the strain.

Thinking into your waist . . . your hips . . . and down into your main thigh muscles, letting tensions drain down and away as you think down towards your knees . . . and on down into your shins and calves . . . allowing those muscles, too, to relax, feel comfortable . . . and let go as you think on into the ankles and down into the feet, into the toes, right the way down to the very tips of the toes . . . All your muscles are relaxed, tension-free and feeling good.

Tense your facial muscles – feel the tension around your eyes and mouth – then let it go.

Clench your fists – feel the tension in your fingers, hands and arms – then let it go.

The Numbers Game – a Meditation for Adults or Children

This is a very simple meditation using a blackboard, real or imaginary. It is a good "game" to use with children, to give them an experience of meditation: they really enjoy it. It is presented as if you are leading a group of children, but it can be easily used by an adult, and is an excellent way to clear the mind through concentration, imagination and patterns, all of which are wonderful ways of gaining a real experience of deep meditation.

1 Get the children to sit or lie comfortably. Once they have found a really comfortable position ask them to remember it, and then sit up, knowing they are going to return to this relaxed position in a few moments.

2 With chalk on the blackboard, draw a diagram of numbers, three lines by three columns, making sure that there are no mathematical links, like this:

3	**1**	**5**
8	**6**	**9**
4	**7**	**2**

3 Give the children one minute, and really show them that you are timing it, to memorize this pattern in lines and columns. They will be working with this later in their mind's eye (that screen on the inside of the forehead).

4 Ask them to return to their relaxed position, eyes closed. Ask them to concentrate on the numbers, and if anything else comes into their mind, to recognize it and then push it away (repeat this often during the session).

5 Rub out lines or columns of numbers, telling the children what you are doing and asking them to do the same in their mind's own diagram . . . do this slowly. Keep the pace of your speech slow too . . . give time for them to adjust, and tell them what is left as a check, for example, "That leaves just four numbers". Continue until they reach the last number. Really concentrate on that number . . . long pause . . .

6 Then rub out the last number, saying "Now concentrate on what is left" . . . Let them remain in silence until you notice a restlessness – this is often three or more minutes.

7 Wake them gently, by speaking in a soft voice becoming louder with an instruction to "Sit up". Ask them what the last number was and for their reactions.

3
6
7
2

THE HAVEN – YOUR OWN SPECIAL PLACE

Once you have managed to achieve complete physical relaxation and calm, allow your mind to enter a place, whether real or imaginary, that is special to you.

Now you can allow your mind to drift . . . drift to a pleasant, peaceful place. A place that you know and where you always feel able to relax . . . completely. A safe . . . secure . . . place . . . where no one . . . and nothing can ever bother you.

It may be a place you have visited on holiday, a beach or a place in the countryside. Or it may be a room . . . a room you have had . . . a room you do have . . . or a room you would like to have . . . an imaginary place. But it is a place where you can always feel able to let go . . . completely . . . a haven, a haven of tranquillity, unique and special to you.

A time and a place, real or imaginary, that is your special meditative place.

In order to help you imagine this place . . . notice first the light: is it bright, natural or dim . . . is there any particular source of light . . . natural or man-made? Notice also the temperature level . . . hot, warm or cool . . . and any particular source of heat. Be aware of the colours that surround you . . . shapes . . . and textures . . . the familiar objects that make that place special.

You can just be there . . . whether sitting, lying or reclining, enjoying the sounds . . . the smells . . . the atmosphere . . . with nobody wanting anything, nobody needing anything and no one expecting or demanding anything from you . . . you can truly relax.

A Guided Visit to a Country House

Imagine that you are visiting a beautiful country house . . . a really beautiful old country house or stately home, on a warm, sunny, summer's afternoon. You are standing on the staircase that leads down into the entrance hall, one of those wide ceremonial types of staircase. And as you look down across the entrance hall, you can just glimpse, through the open doors opposite, a gravel drive, and the sunlight on the gravel. It's a beautiful, sunny, summer's afternoon and there is no one around to trouble or bother you as you stand on that staircase . . .

Now you are moving down the last ten steps to the hallway, relaxing more and more with each step down.

10 Taking one step down, relaxing and letting go . . .

9 Taking another step down, feeling at ease . . .

8 Becoming more relaxed, letting go even more . . .

7 Just drifting deeper . . . and deeper . . . and even deeper down still . . .

6 Becoming calmer . . . and calmer . . . even calmer still . . .

5 Continuing to relax, continuing to let go and feeling good . . .

4 Relaxing even more . . . letting go even more . . .

3 Sinking deeper . . . drifting even further into this welcoming, relaxed state . . .

Walk steadily down the path, aware of the colour, scents and sounds that surround you.

2 Enjoying those good feelings, feelings of inner peace and relaxation . . .

1 Nearly all the way down now, feeling very good . . . beautifully relaxed . . . and **0**.

You are wandering across that hallway now, towards the open doors and the gardens beyond, soaking up the atmosphere of peace and permanence in that lovely old building.

You wander out through the doors and down the stone steps outside . . . and find yourself standing on the gravel drive outside, a wide gravel drive that leads down to the entrance gates.

As you stand there you notice the lush green lawns, so flat and well-clipped . . . and there are shrubs and trees, different shades of green and brown against a clear, blue sky . . . and you can feel the warmth of the sun on your head and shoulders as you enjoy this beautiful summer's afternoon in this lovely old garden. . . . There are flowerbeds with their splashes of colour so carefully arranged and neatly tended. And there's no one else about . . . nobody needing anything, nobody wanting anything and nobody expecting anything from you, so you can enjoy the peace and serenity and solitude of this afternoon in this beautiful garden that's been so well looked after for so many, many years.

A little way down on the right-hand side of the driveway, you notice an ornamental fish pond, the sort of fish pond you only find in the grounds of an old country house or stately home. So you decide to wander down and have a look at those fish, and begin to scrunch your way down that gravel drive, with nothing disturbing the peace and stillness of that afternoon but the scrunch of the gravel as it moves beneath your feet, and the occasional bird song from a long way away, emphasizing the stillness of the air. You are wandering down towards the fish pond, soaking up the atmosphere of this beautiful garden full of flowers and butterflies.

Eventually . . . eventually you find yourself standing near the edge of the fish pond, looking down into that clear, cool, shallow water, just watching those fish . . . large ornamental goldfish of red and gold, black and silver, swimming so easily . . . gliding so effortlessly among the weed, in and out of shadows and around the lily pads. Sometimes they seem almost to disappear behind the weed and shadows, but always they reappear, with their scales catching the sunlight, red, gold, silver or black.

And as you watch those fish your mind becomes even more deeply relaxed . . .

THE WELL

This continues from the previous visualization of the country house and is intended to take you to even deeper levels of meditation. Alternatively, you can use it just on its own to focus the mind beautifully.

. . . As you watch those fish you notice that the centre of the pond is very, very deep, it could be the top of a disused well.

You take from your pocket a silver-coloured coin, and with great care toss that coin so that it lands over the very centre of the pond, and then you watch as it swings down through the water. The ripples drift out to the edges of the pond, but you just watch that coin as it drifts and sinks deeper and deeper through that cool, clear water, twisting and turning; sometimes it seems to disappear as it turns on edge, at other times a face of the coin catches the sunlight and it flashes through the water . . . sinking, drifting deeper and deeper, twisting and turning as it makes its way down . . . Finally it comes to rest at the bottom of the pond, lying on a cushion of soft brown mud, a silver coin in that still, clean water on its own cushion of mud . . .

And you feel as still and undisturbed as that coin, as still and as cool and motionless as that water, enjoying that feeling of inner peace and stillness.

Watch the spreading ripples as the coin lands in the very centre of the pond.

Suggested Meditations: A Stone or Rock

Once you have gained those relaxed feelings associated with meditation, you can use this time by focusing your attention in various ways. You may meditate on an object, for example, in order to gain insights and self-knowledge. Almost any object can be used, but natural ones seem to be most popular.

Its shape, colour and texture . . . age . . . hardness . . . warm . . . cold . . . wet . . . dry . . . weathering . . . gradual change . . . earth . . . mountain . . . boulder . . . rock . . . pebble . . . gravel . . . sand . . . time . . . change . . . adaptation . . . response . . . but always there . . . permanence . . . "you are my rock".

Above: It might be the shape, texture or colour of the rock that appeals, but it is important to choose a rock or stone that feels right for you.

Right: A single piece of rock might be best for meditation, but consider, too, rocks of all shapes and sizes, perhaps in a stream.

A Flower

Choose a flower and place it in front of you. Use your chosen technique to obtain inner attention, then open your eyes and focus upon the flower. You may find a flow of thought developing, or a collection of words building in your mind. Here are examples of each of these ways of meditating, but please remember that your mind can work in many ways, and should be allowed to flow naturally rather than being directed to match this interpretation.

A flower, in full bloom, the colour in the petals, the connection to the stalk, the way each petal is formed, and the differences and similarities there. How natural and beautiful, the shading and subtle changes caused by the light . . . This flower is at its peak of perfection . . . soon the petals will open and then fall . . . a seed pod will develop there . . . the seeds will scatter . . . some will find earth in which to rest and in the natural cycle of things will stay dormant . . . until the time is right . . . The light and temperature trigger new growth . . . a tiny shoot will then develop and grow, emerging from the soil . . . larger leaves will unfold, then a stalk carrying a tiny green bud will emerge, and as this swells through the casing, colours will emerge and the flower bud will emerge . . . This will develop and form into another flower just like this one, and light and shade will allow its true beauty to be enjoyed again.

Natural beauty . . . colour . . . light . . . shade . . . perpetual change . . . the seasons . . . death . . . decay . . . rebirth . . . growth . . . perfection . . . the natural cycle of living things.

Right: Natural perfection is transitory, but is wonderful in its form, colour and beauty.

Above: Focus on an imaginary exotic flower. Below: The natural cycle of birth, growth, death and rebirth.

A flickering candle flame, with its ever-changing light that gives colour, shape and form to all it illuminates, is one of the most popular images to focus on during a meditation session.

A Clock Ticking

The hands of a clock record the passage of time – time never stands still although our perception of time can change. Past – present – future, the clock registers the moments of life moving forward. Focusing on a clock image can be very restful.

The clock ticks . . . the hands move . . . so slowly . . . always moving . . . seconds tick away . . . The one just passed is over . . . a new one takes its place . . . it too is replaced . . . as time moves on . . . Each moment lasts only a second . . . The clock may stop . . . time . . . never stops, it moves on . . . The moment that is over is out of reach . . . the moment to come has not arrived, yet . . . this moment is MINE . . . this moment I can use as I wish . . . I focus on this moment . . . I influence this moment . . . I can use this moment . . . and no other NOW!

Measurement . . . movement . . . monitoring . . . invention . . . mechanism . . . complexity . . . regularity . . . cogs . . . gears . . . chains . . . weights . . . pendulum . . . interaction . . . perpetual motion . . . never still . . . always moving . . . key . . . battery heart.

Hold an image of a clock face in your mind and imagine the hands slowly moving around the face.

A Picture

This can be a way of bringing the outside world into your meditation, or coming to an understanding of another person's view of the world. Select a picture, religious or otherwise, and having gained a meditative state, allow yourself to focus that acute attention upon the picture and let your thoughts flow. They may be about the total picture, or one aspect of it, or the making of the picture and what was intended by its creator. Let your mind do the work for you, and you can be sure that it will be utilizing the picture to stimulate insights that are helpful and relevant to your needs at that moment.

A picture tells a story – the story as depicted by the artist or photographer, the story as seen and interpreted by the world of the viewer. One picture can tell many stories – all different – all are the interpretations of the viewer's mind at the moment of viewing.

Using the Meditative State:

Leaving Troubles Behind

This meditation, which is known as the "railway tunnel", is particularly helpful in leaving troubles behind, gaining perspective and focusing on the here and now, uncluttered by past concerns.

Imagine yourself strolling along a very straight flat path. It's a dull, cloudy, drizzly sort of day, the path is leading between two high banks, there is damp grass beneath your feet, and you can see the cloudy sky above. Somehow you feel heavy, you are aware of a heavy back-pack on your shoulders, making your steps heavy and slow. Your back is bent a little to support the weight and you seem to be looking at the ground in front of you as you trudge along the path, feeling damp and cold and weighed down. You glance up and see the entrance to an old railway tunnel: this must be a disused railway line. As you look, you can see a point of light at the other end of the tunnel, so it cannot be too long. You decide to continue on your walk; at least you will be out of the drizzle in there. As you approach the entrance, the tunnel seems very dark, but that small circle of light at the far end is reassuring so you keep moving forward into the tunnel . . . At first it seems very dark, you can hardly see at all, but the floor feels even and it is easy to walk along. As you do so, all those old doubts about yourself begin to surface in your mind; you are aware of your own failings and those things you wish you hadn't done, and indeed the things you wish you had done in the past . . . Just let them come gently to the surface of your mind. The back-pack seems to be getting a little lighter as these different doubts and regrets unpack from your inner mind, gently and easily. You keep walking, and notice a pool of light on the floor ahead . . . there must be an air shaft there. As you go through the pool of light you suddenly remember a happy time, when someone really enjoyed your company, a time when you felt really good about being you. As you move out of the light into the darkness again you feel lighter still, the back-pack is emptying and you are standing a little straighter now, but the doubts are rising to the surface, the regrets are floating up into your mind again. The circle of light at the end of the tunnel is getting bigger now, but here is another air shaft, with that shaft of light penetrating the gloom of the tunnel. Again, as you pass through that light, another good memory of being appreciated for who you are, being praised for something, or complimented, comes to the forefront of your mind. Now you are back in the gloom, but it doesn't seem as intense as before. It is getting lighter and warmer step by step now, and more and more good memories of those who have loved you and events that pleased you come into your mind . . . As you get nearer to the end of the tunnel you notice that the sun must be shining because it all looks very bright out there, and you find that you feel so much lighter, as if you have lost that back-pack altogether now, and a pleasant warmth is beginning to replace any traces of damp and cold that you felt before.

Eventually you step out into the bright summer sunshine, and smell the aroma of freshly cut grass, and walk out with a light tread into the warmth of a bright summer's day, feeling lighter and valuing yourself and the world around you much more. You realize you have still so many opportunities and possibilities awaiting you and new chances to do things that make you feel good about yourself, and at ease with others. Your contribution is important, and you are a valuable and lovable human being.

Focus on the fluidity of clouds as they slowly disperse.

Walk out of the tunnel into a brighter, lighter world.

Meditation for Personal Development and Growth Affirmations

Affirmations are a deceptively simple device that can be used by anyone and have proved remarkably effective. You should try to use this method while in the meditative state, having previously planned and memorized the affirmations involved. Thus, you combine ease of communication with all parts of the mind and the effectiveness of repeated powerful positive phrases. The technique requires you to say to yourself, out loud, a positive statement about yourself as you wish to be: examples are given later.

To make affirmations effective, they should
- be made in the present tense
- be positively phrased
- have an emotional reward.

If you notice what happens if you are asked not to think of elephants, you will realize why negatives (the words "no", "not", "never" and so on) will have the opposite effect to that intended. Yours is the most influential voice in your life, because you believe it! Be aware of any negative statements you regularly make about yourself, either to others or to yourself – "I am shy," "I lack confidence," "I cannot," "I get nervous when" and so on – they are self-limiting beliefs that you are reinforcing each time they slip into your conversation or mind. Now you can use affirmations while meditating to change those beliefs.

Right: Affirmations change the way you think about yourself and the way you act and react.

VISUALIZATION

In the same way that you can utilize your voice, so, perhaps more powerfully, you can use your imagination. The imagination can stimulate emotions, and these can register new attitudes in the mind. It can be a direct communication with the deeper levels of the mind and can provide a powerful influence for improvements in your attitudes, behaviour patterns and overall confidence.

Visualization requires that you imagine yourself in a situation, behaving, reacting and looking as you would wish to do at an interview, an important meeting, a social gathering, a one-to-one situation, or perhaps a sporting event. Imagine what that will mean for you, your reactions, the reactions of those around you and, importantly, feel all the good feelings that will be there when this happens in reality.

It is like playing a video of the event, on that screen on the inside of the forehead, the mind's eye, from the beginning of the situation through to the perfect outcome for you. Should any doubts or negative images creep into your "video", push them away and replace them with positive ones. Keep this realistic, and base it upon real information from your past. Once you are happy with the images you are seeing, note the way you are standing and presenting yourself. Then allow yourself to "climb aboard", and view the scene from inside your imagined self. Now you can get in touch with the feelings and attitudes that make the event successful. The best time to do this is when relaxed mentally and physically – during meditation. Teach yourself to expect new, positive outcomes. This can be combined with affirmations, to make it doubly effective.

Rehearse the forthcoming event in your mind's eye so that you are fully prepared.

Improved Self Worth

We all have attributes and qualities in which we can take pride and pleasure. This exercise is about emphasizing these positive aspects to allay the doubts that only serve to limit our potential.

- I like my [physical attribute]
- I am proud of my [attitude or achievement]
- I love meeting people – they are fascinating
- My contribution is valuable to [name person]
- I am lovable and can give love
- Others appreciate my [opinions, assistance, a personal quality]
- I enjoy being a unique combination of mind and body

Imagine yourself speaking to colleagues, boss, employees or friends . . . See yourself behaving and looking confident, standing and looking a confident person . . . Notice how you stand . . . your facial expression . . . hear the way that you speak . . . slowly, calmly, quietly, clearly and with

Right: Value yourself and acknowledge your own positive features and qualities.

Above: Be aware of how you stand, your facial expressions and the feelings involved.

confidence. You are communicating your needs . . . ideas . . . opinions in a positive way. Notice how your words flow easily, and how others are listening attentively to you . . . valuing what you have to say. Now "climb aboard" . . . be there – know how it feels to stand like that . . . to speak like that . . . and to have that positive reception from others. Get in touch with the stance . . . expression . . . and feelings . . . and know that you can use these any time in the future to gain those same feelings or inner strength supporting you in everything you do.

See yourself in different situations: at home, in a social setting, in all the parts of your life, being a confident, self-assured person. You are valuing your own talents, and the inner strengths that come from experience . . . knowledge . . . skills . . . insights . . . understanding . . . attitudes . . . patterns of behaviour . . . strengths that support you in everything you do.

Above: Always try to be open with others so that they feel able to be open with you.

FOR INSTANT RELAXATION

Having trained yourself to meditate and to gain those feelings of focused attention combined with physical relaxation, you can utilize the "triggers" you have been using to gain the same feeling of relaxation at any time. If you have been imagining being in a certain place, doing so will instantly give you those feelings, or if you have been using a trigger word the same is true.

It may be that you are aware of certain physical symptoms during meditation, such as a tingling in the hands or feet: this too may be a useful trigger. Imagine that you feel those symptoms and you will gain the sensations and feelings associated with meditation within seconds. This can be especially useful before an important meeting, or any occasion about which you may be feeling a little apprehensive, in order to gain the calm confidence you need and to put things into their proper perspective.

Your mind has accepted the training and linkages you have created during meditation, and will respond to the same signals or triggers at any time, quickly and easily, for all the benefits that come with the practice of meditation.

Left: Meditation is excellent for recharging the batteries and rediscovering vitality, energy and well-being.
Right: A tropical beach with all its beauty, warmth and tranquillity provides a lovely mental image to focus on during meditation.

For Confidence in Future Situations

The meditative state, affirmations and visualization can be a valuable rehearsal and preparation for a future event. Athletes and other sports people have proved that it works. We can all use this process to achieve our own optimum performance in any situation.

- I am quietly confident in meetings
- I speak slowly, quietly and confidently so that others listen
- My contribution is wanted and valued by others
- I enjoy meetings, as they bring forth new ideas and renew my enthusiasm

Imagine a meeting that is about to happen, and see yourself there, filling in all the details that you know, and the people too; imagine yourself there looking confident and relaxed, concentrating on what is happening. Be aware of the acute interest you are giving to what is happening, complete, concentrated attention, and then imagine yourself speaking, to give information or to ask a question: hear yourself speaking quietly, slowly and calmly . . . Notice people listening to what you are saying; they wish you well and support you, as you are expressing your viewpoint or raising a question they may well have wanted to ask, too. Notice how you are sitting or standing, how you lean slightly forward when speaking . . . that expression of calm confidence on your face. When this is clear in your mind, just like a film playing in your mind's eye, play it back and forth. When you are feeling comfortable with it, get into that imaginary you, "climb aboard" and be there in your mind, seeing things from that perspective, hearing things from that point in the meeting. As you speak, get in touch with those calm feelings, and the attitudes that allow you to feel calm, in control, and quietly confident there . . . It is like a rehearsal; the more you rehearse the better the final performance will be. You will acquire the attitudes, stance and tone of voice, so that when you are in that situation all of these will be available to you, and it will be just as you imagined, as if you had done it all, successfully, before.

Imagine yourself at an important event where you are at ease.

The moment of initial introductions can be tense, but remember how you looked, stood and felt in your visualization.

The preparation was worth it, having given your best and feeling good about your performance.

For Living for Now

Although we cannot change the past, we can learn from it and build up skills and useful insights from it. The future is that unknown world of possibilities and opportunities before us – but all that we can truly have any effect upon is now.

- I have learned a great deal from the past
- The future is an exciting range of opportunities
- I am able to enjoy my acute awareness of this moment
- I am living NOW

The past is over, the future is unknown and so the only time we can truly affect is NOW.

- NOW is the beginning of the rest of my life
- I enjoy laying good foundations NOW on which to build a better future

Imagine yourself standing on a pathway, a pathway that stretches in front of you, and, if you look over your shoulder, trails behind you, the way you have come . . . As you look around, you are aware that the area immediately around you, to the left, right and above, is brilliantly illuminated, and that sounds are amazingly clear. You are acutely aware of all that is happening around you, and your reactions to it. Now that you look ahead again, you see that the path in front is there, but is dim in comparison with the area around you. As you check over your shoulder you notice the path behind is even less clear. You hear a clock chime in the distance and take a step forward, and strangely that bright, acute awareness immediately around you travels with you . . . You notice the slightest of noises, movements or shifts of light, and take pleasure even in the pure sound of silence, too. You can hear

For a complete experience, be more acutely aware of shapes and textures as well as sounds, colours and scents.

that same clock ticking now, and with each tick you can take a small step forward, effortlessly, along the path, and that illumination and awareness moves with you, so that you are constantly acutely aware of the here and now . . . At any fork in the path you can make decisions easily and quickly, as you are truly involved in the moment, rather than looking over your shoulder at what might have been, or staring blindly into the future at what might happen. You enjoy being in the brilliantly illuminated, acute awareness of sound, hearing, feeling, taste and smell that is NOW.

Appreciate the qualities of your food: its colour, shape and aroma, its temperature, texture and flavour.

FOR HEALTH

The mind and body are so completely interlinked that if we keep physically fit we are also mentally alert. Likewise, if we utilize our mental capacities we can affect our physical health and performance, too.

- I feel safe in the knowledge that my body is constantly renewing itself
- It feels good to know that every damaged cell is replaced with a healthy one
- My immune system is strong and fights off any infections easily
- My mind and my body are working in harmony to keep me healthy

Imagine yourself lying or sitting comfortably. As you see yourself there you notice a healing glow of coloured light surrounding your body, but not touching it. Let that colour become stronger, until it has a very clear pure colour, the colour of healing for you.

Now, as you watch, that healing, coloured light begins to flow into the top of your head. You can see it slowly draining into all parts of the head, face, ears, and starts its journey down through the neck and shoulders, into the tops of the arms . . . It continues to flow down through the arms and the chest area, that healing, coloured light, penetrating all the muscles and organs . . . even as you watch you can also feel a healing warmth coming into your body . . . NOW . . . as it flows down into the stomach area, the back, right the way down to the base of the spine. At the same time it is reaching your fingertips too, and that warmth is there in your body right now . . . It continues to flow down through the legs towards the knees, down into the calves and shins, the ankles and on into the feet. All the way into the toes, that healing, coloured light just glows throughout the whole body now.

And now that the whole body is suffused with

Meditation can help free you of physical tension and mental anxiety.

Concentrate on areas of the body that need healing, and imagine yourself free of aches, pains, illness and tension.

Exercise promotes physical fitness and improves mental clarity.

coloured, healing light, and there is a warmth throughout your body, you notice the light concentrating in certain areas, areas that need healing attention. The warmth there seems more obvious as that healing light focuses upon repairing and replacing damaged tissue and focuses your own inner resources to help and heal and bring comfort to that area.

And you feel that area gaining the benefits of that healing light, combined with comfortable warmth. Then you can allow the light to disperse again and gradually return to your normal wakeful state, knowing that in those areas that need it, the healing process will continue to focus your own healing resources into the necessary repair and replacement cycle that is so natural and normal in all living creatures.

Health is a combination of the mind and body.

For Decision Making

If there are alternatives to be considered and a decision to be made, you have an inner adviser who can be helpful. We all have a higher self, made up of a conscience and an ideal self towards which we strive. It is not always possible to get in touch with this important resource while going about our daily business, but when in meditation, in that inner stillness, those inner resources become available.

It may help to imagine your inner advisor as a wise old man or woman, or a bird such as the wise owl.

Some may wish to imagine sitting in front of a wise old man or woman – this may be an image of someone we have known in our life, or a completely imaginary being. Some may choose an animal or a bird, such as an owl, as the focus of attention. Having imagined this inner adviser in whichever way suits you, now imagine being with that adviser and asking a simple question about your problem, then wait . . . You may get a very real insight straight away, or it may be that your adviser uses a present or gives you a scene to think about, or may even open up a possibility not yet considered. At first the answer may seem obscure, but at some later point the meaning will become obvious to you.

We all have an inner adviser, a source of wisdom, formed perhaps before birth, but constantly being brought up to date by our day-to-day experience of the world around us, and our own reactions to it. It is a valuable resource, and with the help of meditation you can use it to give you the confidence to make decisions, and move forward into your future.

Right: You may like to imagine a friend as your inner advisor. Below: Different cultures have adopted particular animals as symbols of wisdom.

FOR REDUCTION OF STRESS

Stress is a factor in everyone's life and can even be a major motivator in some circumstances. Meditation can be a great help in coping with it, and combined with visualization, it can change your whole response to the many stressful demands of modern living.

- I enjoy solving problems
- I work well under pressure
- I am a calm, methodical and efficient worker
- I love that feeling of having achieved so much in a day
- I enjoy being calm when others around me are not

Imagine yourself in a situation that has in the past caused stress. Picture the situation, and the other people involved . . . See yourself there . . . and notice a slight shimmer of light between yourself and those other people . . . a sort of bubble around you . . . a protective bubble that reflects any negative feelings back to them . . . leaving you able to get on with your tasks . . . your life, with an inner strength and calmness that surprises even you. A protective, invisible bubble surrounds you at all times. It will only allow those feelings that are positive and helpful to you to pass through for you to enjoy and build upon. Others may catch stress from each other . . . negativity, too, can be infectious . . . but you are protected . . . you continue to keep things in perspective . . . and to deal with things calmly and methodically. You are able to see the way forward clearly . . . solve problems . . . find ways around difficulties . . . by using your own inner resources and strengths, born of experience.

Now see yourself talking to someone who has been causing pressure to build. Find yourself knowing just how to let them know that what they are doing, or saying, is unhelpful in resolving the problem or difficulty. Find yourself able to let them know in such a way that they can accept without offence . . . and find your own calmness and control . . . a strength that supports you. You can let someone know if too much is being expected, and explain why. See yourself in that situation . . . calmly explaining the areas of difficulty . . . being able to supply examples and information until they understand the position. At all times you are surrounded by that protective bubble of light that keeps you calm and quietly confident, thinking everything through clearly and explaining it simply to others.

Next, imagine pushing out through that same protective bubble emotions that are unhelpful . . . past resentments . . . and hurts . . . embarrassments, too. You push them out through the bubble . . . where they can no longer limit or harm you. You are now better able to control the way you feel and react . . . The bubble stays with you and enables you to remain in control . . . keeping things in perspective . . . having the strength to change those things you can change . . . accept those things that you cannot . . . and move on!

Left: Your protective bubble will stay with you always whatever you do. Right: Always try to see things how they really are rather than allowing problems or difficulties to be distorted or magnified by worry.

For Improved Concentration and Study Skills

The pressures that are experienced when studying for an examination can actually disrupt concentration and so one's ability to learn and remember information. Meditation in this visual form can re-energize the ability to learn.

- I enjoy those moments of insight and understanding
- I enjoy using my mind and expanding the boundaries of my knowledge
- My memory is expanding with new information
- My learning ability improves with use
- I concentrate so completely that nothing but an emergency can distract me

Imagine a huge jigsaw spread out in front of you: it is a giant picture made up of many smaller images, and each image is a jigsaw in itself. Some images are nearly complete, others are only just starting to form, some even seem a confused jumble of unattached pieces. Focus your attention on one image, just one part of the giant jigsaw, one that is nearly complete but is still a little confusing – you are still not quite sure what the image will turn out to be.

A new piece comes into your hand, and you see that it fits, it fills a gap as it interlocks with all the surrounding pieces . . . The image suddenly becomes clear, and you can see it now. You have a wonderful feeling of achievement, for something that was unclear is now clear; that which was confusing is now fully understood. You feel just as you do when a new piece of information interlocks with other information and you understand the whole subject. That insight . . . that moment of learning . . . the joy of understanding is what makes learning so worthwhile.

Should you ever need to retrieve that piece of the jigsaw, to answer a question of some kind, you know . . . you know that it is there . . . and all the interlocking pieces that together give insight and understanding are all there all the time for you to select and use when you need them.

The memory is like a giant jigsaw, and the moments of achievement when understanding and enlightenment take place are the joy of learning itself.

As you enjoy learning, so you enjoy total concentration as you study, take notes and engross yourself in the process of learning. It is, for that study period, as if nothing else matters but exercising your intelligence in the process of gaining information, skills and insight, and expanding the capabilities of your mind. Only an extreme emergency could distract you. Learning is a continuous part of being alive.

For Goal Achievement

A goal, in all areas of life, is important in order to focus one's attention and inner resources. A goal provides a sense of direction and ultimately the joy of achievement.

- I direct my energies to achieve my goals
- I enjoy directing my energies positively
- I know where I am going and how I am getting there
- Step by step I am moving in the right direction
- I have the ability, I have the determination, I shall succeed

Be aware of the different areas of your life; work, social, leisure activities, emotional and spiritual. Select one of these for this exercise . . . and be aware of what you want to happen in that area of your life, what you want to achieve . . . Make it realistic and clear in your mind. It may be useful to write it down, and describe it fully before beginning this visualization.

While in the meditative state, imagine yourself having achieved that goal, imagine yourself there, in that situation. Surround yourself with all the things or people that indicate that you have achieved that goal. Be as specific as you can . . . be aware of all the senses . . . what are you seeing . . . hearing . . . touching or sensing . . . smelling . . . tasting. Be there . . . make it real . . . be specific . . . about colours . . . temperatures . . . lighting, to make it more and more real in your mind.

Be there and know how it feels to have achieved that goal . . . Be aware of how it makes you feel . . . how it affects your mood . . . and your feeling about yourself.

Now, from where you are at that moment of achieving that goal . . . look back . . . as if along a path, a pathway of time . . . to where you were . . . and notice the different stages of change . . . of movement towards achieving that goal . . . along the way . . . along that path . . . the different actions you have

taken . . . the contacts you have made . . . and the people involved. Be aware of the smallest moments of change that have happened from where you were to this moment of having achieved your goal . . . from the start of the journey to its fulfilment . . . Be aware of all the stages along the way . . . and as you return to the here and now . . . you remain in touch with the feelings that will make it all worthwhile . . . and you feel more and more determined to take one step at a time . . . make one change at a time . . . along that path to the successful achievement of your goal.

And as you return from the meditative state . . . as you return to full wakefulness . . . so you are more and more determined to be successful in the achievement of your goal and to take the first step towards it, today.

Below and left: One step at a time and eventually you will reach your goal and enjoy the view and the feeling of success.

FOR IMPROVED CREATIVITY

Many adults have a craving to be creative but underestimate their ability to be so. Creativity takes many forms and everyone is creative in some way or another. Use these exercises to rediscover your latent creativity and rebuild your confidence in your skills and talents.

- I enjoy my own creativity
- I am blessed with a vivid imagination
- I love to express myself in creative ways
- I enjoy my own imaginative responses to the world as I see and feel it

Imagine yourself in a wonderful room . . . a room surrounded by windows looking out on to countryside . . . In this room there are many small areas, and you can move freely around the room trying each of the areas to see how you feel . . . Here on the left is a large piece of paper with pens and pencils, a small studio for drawing and sketching . . . Another area has an easel and paints set out ready for you, the artist, to take up . . . Another has clay for you to handle and form into shapes or pots . . . Another has a word processor ready for your fingers to create images in poetry or prose . . . Yet another has many engineering tools for the inventor . . . Another has cameras and photographic equipment . . . Just spend some time moving around and trying them all . . . these are just some of the areas into which you may choose to channel your own creativity, and where no one else need judge or approve. Only your opinion matters, and the joy of translating the inner world of the imagination into a form or expression that suits you . . . Which feels most stimulating, most exciting, and most comfortable?

Become more and more aware that everyone has a creative ability, to tell stories, to create beauty, to capture a moment . . . Imagine yourself using one of the

Inspiration can come in many forms: natural or man-made; real or imaginary.

Left: There are so many different ways to express one's creativity. Below: Children are naturally creative and that creativity remains with us into adulthood. It is there within us just waiting to be rekindled.

areas in this marvellous room, or indeed finding another area not yet described . . . in order to create your response to the world around you, or your inner world. Be aware of the feeling of having time and energy to channel into this creative activity. Be aware of the focus of attention that this creates for you; nothing else seems to matter . . . but the ability to utilize your innate creativity . . . and the joy that comes when something tangible forms in front of you. For many the process is more exciting than the end product – which gives you the greater satisfaction?

Sometimes we drive smoothly and happily along a road, we come to traffic lights on red and have to pause. The creative flow can be like that too, but the lights turn to amber and then green and off we go, just as you will when that temporary block dissolves . . . Enjoy your creativity and imaginative power, and translate it into the world around you. You know that you can do it, for your own sake, for its sake, free of the need to please anyone else but yourself.

INDEX

Photography Credits
The publishers would like to credit the following: Bruce Coleman Collection: Steven J Doyle, 8; Kim Taylor, 34; Stephen Bond, 41; Imagebank: Anselm Spring, 9; Marc Romanelli, 10; Juan Silva, 11; J. Carmichael, 23; S. Achernar, 47; Visual Arts Library 35, 39; Simon Bottomley 3, 13, 46, 51b, 53br; Michelle Garrett 5, 36, 51t; Don Last 14, 17, 21, 24, 26, 27, 49, 53tl, 55, 57; Debbie Patterson 25, 33, 37; John Freeman 31; Alistair Hughes 53tr; James Duncan 63. t=top, b=bottom, l=left, r=right